Learning To Slow Down and Pay Attention

A Book For Kids About ADD

2nd Edition

By

Kathleen G. Nadeau, Ph.D. and Ellen B. Dixon, Ph.D.

Illustrated by John Rose

Magination Press • Washington, DC

Library of Congress Cataloging-in-Publication Data

Nadeau, Kathleen G.
　　Learning to slow down and pay attention: a book for kids about
　　ADD / by Kathleen G. Nadeau and Ellen B. Dixon; illustrated by John
　　Rose. — 2nd ed.
　　　　p.　cm.
　　Includes bibliographical references (p.　).
　　ISBN 1-55798-456-5
　　　　1. Attention-deficit hyperactivity disorder—Juvenile literature.
　　2. Attention-deficit-disordered children—Juvenile literature.
　　I. Dixon, Ellen B.　II. Title.
　　RJ506.H9N33　1997
　　618.92'8589—dc21　　　　　　　　　　　　　　　　　　96-52304
　　　　　　　　　　　　　　　　　　　　　　　　　　　　CIP
　　　　　　　　　　　　　　　　　　　　　　　　　　　　AC

Published by
MAGINATION PRESS
An Educational Publishing Foundation Book
American Psychological Association
750 First Street, NE
Washington, DC 20002

Manufactured in the United States of America
10 9 8 7 6 5 4 3 2

ACKNOWLEDGMENTS

We would like to express our appreciation to the many parents and children who have shared their experiences with us and helped us to develop the ideas for this book. In this second edition, we would also like to thank the children who have used this book and who have helped us learn ways to improve it. We would especially like to thank the little boy who told us that he slept with our book at night because "this book understands me." We tried hard to write a book that "understands" kids with attentional problems, and we hope that our second edition "understands" an even broader group of children.

Our grateful thanks go to Patricia Quinn, M.D., developmental pediatrician and nationally recognized specialist in ADD, who shared her expertise, and who took time from her busy schedule to offer suggestions, encouragement, and editorial input for our first edition. We are also indebted to Melvin D. Levine, M.D., of the Clinical Center for the Study of Development and Learning at the University of North Carolina at Chapel Hill, who gave the valuable suggestion to minimize the use of labels, which can be both divisive and damaging, and to focus instead on issues and solutions.

Another invaluable contributor to this book has been our cartoonist, John Rose. He worked long and patiently with us to develop cartoon characters which would be both appealing to children and accurately representative of the struggles that children with attentional problems face. His cartoons engage children, drawing them to the book, and leading them to read it repeatedly—exactly what needs to happen in order for children to understand and remember.

Finally, we would like to extend our thanks to Beverly Horn who has worked with us for many years, patiently and painstakingly, translating our various scribbles through countless drafts, both in the original book, the revised edition, and now, through this second edition.

INTRODUCING
THIS SECOND EDITION

We've kept many things the same in this second edition of *Learning to Slow Down and Pay Attention* because we've gotten lots of positive feedback from parents, from other professionals, and from the kids themselves.

In this second edition, however, we have added a number of things that make the book more helpful, we hope, and more appropriate for a broader range of children. Parents and professionals will note that there are many additions to our "Things I Can Do To Help Myself" section designed to give a positive message to kids about "taking charge" of their ADD behaviors.

Most importantly, the changes reflect the growing acknowledgment that there are many non-hyperactive children with attentional difficulties who are less likely to be diagnosed, and less likely to be referred by parents or teachers. Hyperactive kids tend to create many more "squeaking wheels" than non-hyperactive ones. We hope that the changes in our second edition will be helpful to these children who are easily overlooked, and will lead more parents and professionals to identify and understand them.

Although we included girls in our first edition, we have given girls a greater emphasis in this second edition, highlighting some of the differences in the problems girls experience.

We hope that you like our changes, and we'd love to hear from parents, professionals, and kids with your reactions to our second edition of *Learning to Slow Down and Pay Attention: A Book for Kids About ADD*.

TO PARENTS
AND OTHER ADULT HELPERS

We've divided this book into four parts: 1) A Checklist About Me!, 2) Things Other People Can Do to Help Me, 3) Things That I Can Do to Help Myself, and 4) Special Projects With Your Mom or Dad.

We suggest that you read the book along with your child and that you go through only one section at a sitting, pausing to discuss various points and ideas wherever this seems useful. The third section, which focuses on things children can learn to do to help themselves, should be used repeatedly as a resource while children gradually build skills in these areas. We've added some new ways for children to help themselves in our pages on making friends, cleaning up a bedroom, managing the fidgets, etc. Finally, in the back of this edition, we have added a section on ways parents and kids can work together on projects and habits. At the end of each section is an activity that we hope will end the session on a relaxed and upbeat note for your child.

You may notice as you read this book with your child that we have avoided the ADD or ADHD label in the text for children. We have done this for several reasons. As more and more research is done with both children and adults, we realize that we are dealing with a very complex set of neuro-developmental issues, which are inadequately described by the ADHD label. There is a great deal of variety among children who are currently labeled ADHD. Other children who manifest significant attentional difficulties do not meet the strict criteria for an ADHD diagnosis, and yet these children are in great need of assistance and intervention. By avoiding the label, we can address the needs of all children with problems of attention, concentration, impulsivity, or hyperactivity.

Just as importantly, we don't want to suggest to children that they have a "disease" called "ADHD." What children need is to gain an understanding of their particular problems with attention, impulsivity, and hyperactivity and what can be done to assist them.

We hope this new edition will be an enjoyable way for your child to learn about him or herself and to begin the life-long process of self-understanding and self-help.

Kathleen Nadeau and Ellen Dixon

Contents

Acknowledgments.. iii

Introducing This Second Edition iv

To Parents and Other Adult Helpers v

Introduction: Just for Kids! 1

Part One: A Checklist About Me! 5

    At School.. 6

    With My Friends 8

    About Myself... 10

    At Home.. 12

    What I Wish Other People Knew........................... 14

Part Two: Things That Other People
**   Can Do To Help Me................................ 19**

Part Three: Things I Can Do To Help Myself........ 25

    Ways to Remember 26

    Getting Ready in the Morning 28

    The Easy Way to Clean up a Bedroom................. 30

    Ways to Pay Better Attention at School............... 32

    Things to Do If You Feel Fidgety......................... 34

    Homework.. 36

    Learning to Control Your Anger........................... 38

    Learning to Ask for Help...................................... 42

    Learning to Talk Out Problems at Home 44

    Problem Solving 46

    Learning Not to Interrupt...................................... 48

Try These Ways to Make and Keep Friends 50

Things to Do When Someone Hurts
  Your Feeling 52

Ways to "Feel Good About Me" 54

Learning to Relax 56

When You Have Trouble Going to Sleep 58

Things I Want to Change 60

**Part Four: Special Projects with
  Your Mom or Dad 61**

Notes to Parents 67

ADD Organizations for Parents 69

Suggested Reading 70

About the Authors 72

INTRODUCTION

Just for Kids!

Our names are Kathleen Nadeau and Ellen Dixon. We are psychologists who work with boys and girls. Some of the kids we work with have trouble paying attention in school or finishing their homework. Some of them are very active and have trouble sitting still in school all day. For other kids it is hard to remember to do things or to remember things they have been told. Some of these kids get in trouble because they do things before they stop and think.

If you have any of these difficulties, we hope that this book can help you understand more about yourself and about some of the things that can help you. If you are like this, probably someone else in your family is like this, too—maybe your mom, your dad, or an aunt or uncle. These traits usually run in families. Your brain may work in a slightly different way that makes it harder for you to pay attention, to listen, and to remember.

There are lots of things that can help with these kinds of problems. Some things you can learn to do for yourself. Other things can be done by your parents, your teachers, your doctor, or your counselor. We'd like you to read this book with your parents so that you can talk to them about what you read. We hope you like it and that it helps you.

Let us know what you think. We'd love to hear from you after you read this book. There are lots of books for parents and teachers, but we thought that kids deserved to have their own book. So this one is just for you!

Lots of kids, and grown-ups, too, have trouble paying attention. Some kids are always running around with lots of energy. It's almost like their motor runs too fast and can't turn off.

They just blurt things out without thinking and interrupt people all the time. They have trouble paying attention, are wiggly and fidgety, and can't sit still for a long time, like this …

Other kids have trouble paying attention because they're usually thinking about something else and don't notice what goes on around them. They are quiet and daydream a lot. They sit at their desk and try to pay attention, but pretty soon they start thinking about something else, like this...

Do you think you are more fidgety and talkative, or are you a daydreamer? You could be a little of both. What does your mom or dad think? Whether you're active or quiet, you could have trouble with paying attention, being organized, remembering, and keeping track of what is happening.

We've talked to lots of kids with these kinds of problems, but no two kids are exactly alike. The next section of our book tells you some of the things that these kids have said about themselves. We would like you to read each comment with your mom or dad. Make a check mark in the box next to each comment that you think is just like you.

Like this:

After you have finished checking off the things that are like you, the next parts of the book will tell you how to improve some of these difficulties and how other people can help you.

Part One

A Checklist
About Me

Teachers are always telling me,
   "Slow down, don't rush!"

When I'm at school, it's hard to
   sit still at my desk.

I forget to raise my hand.

I can't seem to get organized.

I have trouble getting started on
   my work in class.

My desk is usually a big mess.

I forget to hand in my homework.

I usually forget the directions the
   teacher gives us.

Even when I try to listen, sometimes
   I start daydreaming.

I bother other kids too much.

Sometimes I get in trouble for talking.

with my friends...

I get mad too easily when I
  play with my friends.

I don't know why, but a lot of times other
  kids don't want to play with me.

Sometimes other kids complain about
  me to the teacher.

Most of my friends are younger than I am.

I'm not very good at making friends.

My mom or dad tells me I'm too bossy
  with other kids.

Some kids in my class pick on me and
  tease me.

I wish I had more friends.

It's easy to make friends at first, but pretty soon they're not my friends anymore.

about myself...

Sometimes I think I'm not as smart as other kids.

I want the other kids to like me more.

I wish I didn't get so hyper.

Sometimes I think something is wrong with me, but I don't know what.

I wish I didn't get upset so easily.

I get confused a lot, especially at school.

It would be great if I could remember stuff better.

I do dumb things without thinking.

No matter how hard I try, somebody still gets mad at me.

Sometimes I feel different from the other kids.

at home...

Sometimes when I'm playing, I don't hear my parents call me.

I have too many fights with my brother or sister.

It feels like I get in trouble more than anyone else.

I usually finish dinner before everybody else, and I want to get up from the table.

I make mistakes, and then my parents get mad at me.

I hate to do homework.

My room is a big mess.

I have trouble falling asleep at night.

I am sent to "time out" a lot.

12

It feels like I'm always in trouble for something.

what I wish other people knew

I really *do* care about my schoolwork.

I'm not getting in trouble on purpose.

I don't mean to be bossy.

I hate it when people tell me I'm not trying.

Lots of the time it's really confusing to be me.

I want my mom and dad to be proud of me.

Now you've checked off all the things that describe you. Some kids check off almost all of the items. Other kids check off only some of them.

It may feel like you've checked off a lot of problems in this section, but ...

Many other kids have these problems, too. The rest of our book tells about how other people can help you and how you can help yourself.

Now, if you're like a lot of the kids who helped us write this book, you're getting a little tired right now. That's OK. You need a break after you concentrate on listening or reading. (Whenever you're doing school-work, you will get more done if you give yourself a break after about 15 or 20 minutes.)

Why don't you take a break now and see if you can help our heroes find their homework. We bet you know how they feel!

feel better after your break?

That's a good habit to learn. Work for a while. Then take a short break.

Now that you have read this far, you and your mom or dad probably have a pretty good idea of whether or not you are like some of the kids in this book.

To really know whether you need special help, you should have an "evaluation." The evaluation is kind of fun. You and your parents will answer questions like the ones in this book. You might put puzzles together, play memory games, and do all sorts of stuff. If you have already been evaluated, then this book is *definitely* for you!

Now, let's look at ways that your parents and other people can help you learn to pay better attention.

Part Two

Things That Other People Can Do To Help Me

Someone who really understands your problems might go to your school and talk to your teacher about ways to help you to become a better student.

For some kids, it helps to work in a quieter place, or to go to a school with smaller classes. When there are fewer distractions, kids can concentrate better.

Sometimes it is helpful for kids to see a counselor who teaches them how to make friends and how to get along better with other kids. You can tell your counselor about problems you have at home or at school. The counselor never fusses at you and never says it's all your fault.

Counseling can help you understand yourself better and feel more confident about yourself, too. If you go to counseling, it would be a good idea to take this book with you. You could show your counselor the things you checked off in the first section of this book, and your counselor could help you figure out what to do.

Your parents might talk with a special teacher or counselor, too. The counselor can teach your parents better ways to help you get ready for school in the morning, easier ways to help you finish your homework, and better ideas for helping you when you feel angry or frustrated.

Your parents will also learn that you haven't been just lazy or bad. They'll learn that you really have been trying, but that it's hard for you to do what everybody wants you to do.

Some kids go to a doctor who gives them special medicine that helps them calm down, pay better attention, and get their schoolwork done. The medicine used most often is called Ritalin. Taking medicine doesn't mean you are sick. The medicine just gives your body what it needs to help you pay attention and stay on track.

As you can see, there are lots of different ways that other people can help you. But you can also do lots of things to help yourself. On the following pages are some ideas that you can try at home or at school. You'll need to talk about them with your parents and your teacher so that they can help you.

But now you are probably ready for another break.

CONNECT THE DOTS, AND YOU WILL SEE WHY HE'S AS PLEASED AS HE CAN BE!

Part Three

Things I Can Do
To Help Myself

ways to remember...

- Write yourself a note. Colored stick pads are great because you can stick notes where you will be sure to see them.

- It can be hard to remember things you're told. Ask your mom or dad to write you a note and stick it where you'll see it.

- Always put things in the same place: a hook for your jacket, a shelf for books and backpack, a box for shoes, soccer balls, etc. If these are all together in a convenient place, you can easily put your things away when you come in the house.

- Set the kitchen timer as a reminder. For example, if you need to leave for swimming practice in 20 minutes, set the timer to remind you when to go.

- Learn to DO IT NOW! When you think of something, do it right away. Then you won't have time to forget!

- If you need to take something to school, put it in one special place by the door.

- Learn to stop and think for a minute before you rush out the door. "Let's see, have I got everything I need?"

- Think about your day when you wake up. "Let's see, today is Tuesday, so I have soccer practice after school. I need to take my soccer cleats."

getting ready in the morning!

The best way to get ready in the morning is to prepare as much as you can the night before. That way, if something is lost, you'll have time to look for it.

- Put out your clothes the night before.

- Pack your lunch the night before.

- Get together everything you'll need to take to school the next day, like lunch money, homework, and permission slips.

- In the morning, have a regular routine. Doing things in the same order each morning makes it easier to get it done.

- Make a checklist of what to do each morning and put it on the wall where you will see it.

- Don't play or watch TV until you're completely ready!

- Get your mom or dad to set up a "launching pad." This is a place for you to put everything you'll take to school the next day. Make a list near your launching pad of what you'll need.

The easy way To clean a bedroom...

8 STEPS TO A CLEAN ROOM!

You will need:

- A trash can
- 4 cardboard boxes with labels
- A clothes hamper
- Two hooks in your closet
- Some shelves
- A desk

1. Put all the dirty clothes in the clothes hamper and clean clothes in your dresser.
2. Put all the toys on the shelves and in a big cardboard box labeled "toy box."
3. Put all the books in a pile on a shelf or in a cardboard "book box."
4. Put all the school stuff and backpack on your desk or in your cardboard "school box."
5. Put all the trash and throw-away stuff in the trash can or a garbage bag.
6. Put all the shoes in your closet or in the cardboard "shoe box."
7. Make your bed.
8. Hang your pajamas and your coat on hooks in the closet.

If you do this one step at a time, you'll soon be an expert at cleaning up your own bedroom!

Ways to pay better attention at school ...

- Keep your desk clear, so you're only working on one thing at a time.

- Sit close to the front of the class, and look at your teacher whenever he or she is talking.

- Get involved! Don't just sit there. Ask questions and make comments (after raising your hand, of course).

- Ask to be moved away from kids who talk or bother you, and don't talk when you should be listening.

- To remind yourself to pay attention, wear a rubber band on your wrist and give it a little snap if you start daydreaming.

- If your class is too noisy or distracting while you're trying to work, ask the teacher if you can move your desk or sit in a quiet place.

- Don't bring to school toys or games that will distract you.

- If you don't understand something, ask for help right away.

Things to do if you feel fidgety

- Ask the teacher if you can run an errand or help with something for a few minutes. Then go back to your work.

- Ask if you can keep a koosh ball in your desk to squeeze at times when you're <u>not</u> doing schoolwork. (But <u>*never*</u> toss it or throw it!)

- Ask you mom or dad in advance if you may leave the dinner table as soon as you have eaten.

- Stand up and s—t—r—e—t—ch. Then bend over and touch your toes. Then sit back down. Do this quietly.

- Get some exercise every day—by playing outside, taking a walk with your mom or dad, or going to karate lessons or to sports practice.

- Take a 5-minute break if you're doing homework, or spend a few minutes memorizing things while walking around the table.

- Draw pictures at your desk, *if* you have finished your work.

Homework

Some kids take a long time to finish their homework. Here are some helpful hints to get it done right and to get it done sooner.

- Find a quiet place to do homework that's away from temptations like TV.

- Do your homework when you're not too tired. Some kids do better if they play after school and do their homework after dinner. Other kids are too tired after dinner. Think about the best time for you.

- Pick your best time and place for doing homework, and then make it a habit.

- If you get tired of sitting, try standing up for a minute while you read.

- Some kids learn better if they talk out loud and walk around the room while they memorize things like math facts.

- Reward yourself for finishing your homework. A snack or favorite activity is a great reward to look forward to.

- Don't try to do too much at one time. Work for 15 minutes, take a short break, then work some more.

learning to control your anger

When you're really frustrated and feel like you might "lose it," try the **Calm Down Exercise.** It has three parts.

1. Think of something you like, like listening to music, going to the beach, or riding your bike. Try to get a good picture of this in your mind.

2. Take a deep breath and let it out very *slowly.*

3. Think the words "calm down."

OK, go ahead and try it. First think of something nice. Now take a deep breath and let it out **s–l–o–w–l–y** and think "calm down." Now, do it two more times.

You did it. *Terrific!*

Remember, when you're really angry, you may need to do this at least three times. Then, if you're still angry or frustrated, go find a parent or teacher to help you with your problems.

It helps to practice the **Calm Down Exercise** first when you're not angry. Maybe your mother or father would practice it with you. It might help them, too!

Getting frustrated and angry is a problem for lots of kids. Here are some other things you can do to keep from getting angry or upset.

- Go away from the person you're mad at so things don't get worse.

- Find a quiet place, if you can, to do the **Calm Down Exercise.**

- If someone is trying to make you angry, tell yourself that you're too smart to let them get you in trouble. Go tell your parent or your teacher about the problem.

- Stay away from anyone who picks on you or tries to get you upset.

- If something you're <u>doing</u>, like homework, is frustrating you, ask for help right away, before you get really "fed up."

- If you're angry because you are not allowed to do something you want to do, ask your mom or dad if there's a way you can <u>earn</u> it later.

learning to ask for help...

What do you do when you're confused or when something is too hard for you? Some kids feel embarrassed if they don't know what to do, so they just sit there and don't let anyone know. This just makes the problem worse. It's OK if you catch yourself not listening or not understanding. Just go to your teacher or your mom or dad and say something like:

"I forgot what you asked me to do."

or

"Will you help me with this?"

or

"Will you explain that again?"

or

"Will you show me what you mean?"

Explain to your teacher that you are trying hard. Tell your teacher that one way you help yourself is to make sure you understand what you need to do.

learning to talk out problems at home

Do you feel like your mom or dad is "on your case" all the time? Do problems at home usually turn into arguments? It really helps to find a regular time to talk out problems with your parents. If you have lots of arguments with a brother or sister, this could be a good time to talk about those problems, too.

You should pick a time to talk, to listen, to try to understand, and to look for solutions.

- Everyone should have a chance to say how they feel about the problem.

- No interrupting.

- Don't talk for too long. Say what you think in a few sentences and let other people have their turn.

- Don't blame or call names. You are looking for solutions, not new problems!

- Try to come up with some new ideas. Listen to the ideas of your parents.

- Try new ideas for a few days and then talk again.

If you and your family have a regular problem-solving time, things will probably be a lot calmer and nicer at your house!

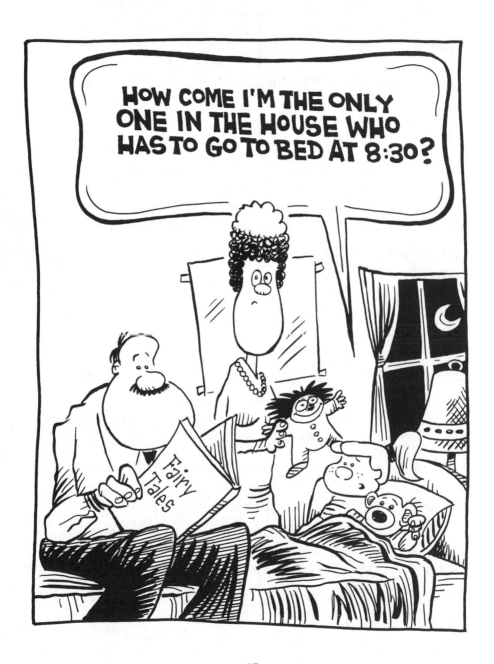

Problem Solving

What do you do when you have a problem? For really big problems you may need the help of a parent or teacher, but sometimes you can figure out what to do all by yourself by using these steps:

Step 1: **What's the problem?**
(For example, forgetting to hand in homework.)

Step 2: **What are some of the things I could do about the problem?**
(I could ask my friend to remind me. I could get a fluorescent folder to put my homework in. I could stick a note on my desk …)

Step 3: **Which one seems best to do?**
(Stick the reminder note on my desk.)

Step 4: **Try out your idea and see if it works.**
(Yeah! I saw my note and handed in my homework!)

Step 5: **If it doesn't work, try another one of your ideas.**

(Oops! I forgot to write the note. Maybe I'll ask Dad to buy me a fluorescent folder to keep my homework in. That way I'll notice the folder and turn in my homework.)

Think of a problem you have now, or that you've had in the past few days. Try "problem solving" using all five steps and see if you can think of a solution you haven't found before. Maybe your mom or dad could help you practice "problem solving."

learning not to interrupt

Some kids have a big problem of interrupting other people. All people interrupt, but some kids interrupt almost constantly. If you do this, the people you are talking to become very annoyed and may even decide they don't want to be friends with you. Here are a few things you can do.

- **Really think about what the other person is saying.** Pretend there will be a quiz in five minutes and you will be asked to repeat every word that person has said.

- **If you have to say something, ask permission.** "Can I say something for just a second?" or "Excuse me, may I ask a question?"

- **If you interrupt, apologize.**

- **Wait until the other person ends his or her sentence before you start talking.**

Not interrupting is something you can practice at home. Make it into a game. See how long you can last at dinner without interrupting.

try these ways to make and keep friends

- Look friendly, smile, and say "Hi."

- Share your stuff when you're playing with friends.

- Take turns. Let everybody get a chance to play with a toy or be a leader.

- Don't be bossy. Let other kids help make decisions.

- Keep calm. Don't get too silly or too loud.

- Say nice things to your friends, like "Good catch!"or "Nice try!"

- Try not to poke, grab, or bump into your friends.

- Don't ever make fun of anybody. You know how awful that feels.

- Don't hit, yell, or call names if you feel angry.

- If you have a big problem, call an adult to help solve it. If you have a little problem, try to work it out with your friend!

things to do when someone hurts your feelings

Some kids' feelings are easily hurt. This can be a big problem, because there are lots of kids who will pick on you even more if they know they can make you get upset. It's never fun to be picked on, but here are a few things that might help:

- **Ignore them.** It's not much fun to pick on someone who doesn't react.

- **Stand up for yourself.** Don't lose your temper, but tell them in a firm voice to "cut it out!"

- **Stay away from them.** If there is a kid at your bus stop who is a bully, for example, it might help to walk to a different bus stop for a while.

- **Talk to a friend or counselor.** When our feelings are hurt, it can really help to talk to someone else about it.

- **Look for kids who are friendly and positive.** Don't keep trying to make friends with someone who is mean or who criticizes you all the time.

ways to "feel good about me"

Some kids start to feel bad about themselves because their teachers and parents criticize them and because they may have problems with other kids. After a while you may feel so discouraged that you think there is nothing good about you. It's really important to feel good about YOU. Here are some things you can do.

- Make a list of things you like about yourself. Ask your mom and dad to add things to your list, too. You can start your list on the next page!

- Look for people who are nice and who encourage you.

- Look for things to do that you can be good at.

- If your mom or dad is critical a lot of the time, this is a good thing to talk about in a family problem-solving session.

- Talk to a counselor about your feelings.

Here's a good place to start your list of things you like about yourself!

_____

_____

_____

_____

_____

_____

_____

_____

learning to relax

Kids sometimes feel very stressed because they are tired, hungry, or have had a hard day at school. These are times when fights and arguments are most likely to happen. When you feel stressed, practice some of these ways to relax! These are good ideas for grown-ups, too!

- Go to your room and lie down or do something quiet.

- Eat a small snack if you are hungry.

- Stay away from your brother or sister if you are fighting with them.

- Take a warm bath.

- Listen to quiet, calm music.

- Take a walk with your mom or dad.

- Curl up with your dog or cat.

when you have trouble going to sleep zzzz

Some kids have a lot of trouble relaxing at night so that they can fall asleep. This can be a big problem. If you have trouble sleeping at night, you will be tired the next day. When you are tired, your difficulties with paying attention, remembering, and doing your school-work will be worse!

Here are some things that can help you fall asleep more easily.

- Have a very regular evening schedule.

- Do things in the same order. For example:

  1. Eat a snack.
  2. Do homework.
  3. Watch a half hour of television.
  4. Eat dinner.
  5. Take a bath, brush your teeth.
  6. Get into bed.
  7. Read a book or magazine.
  8. Good night hug and kiss from your parents.
  9. Lights out.

- Don't do anything really active or exciting on school nights.

- Play soft music after your light is turned off.

- Don't watch TV or listen to your favorite rock station. That will just keep you up longer.

- Try reading a homework assignment. That can sometimes make you go to sleep in 5 minutes!

- Don't take naps during the day or sleep late in the morning. That makes it hard to get to sleep on time at night.

- If you are taking stimulant medicine to help you pay better attention, make sure you don't take it too late in the day.

Things I want to change...

Boy, that's a lot of stuff to try and learn how to do!

Yes it is! We've talked about lots of different things you can do to make your life happier and go more smoothly. Don't expect to learn how to do all of these things at once. You and your parents should decide upon one thing to change. Practice it for a while. When that change is easy for you, then start working on a new one.

Make a list here of things you want to change first.

_____

_____

_____

_____

_____

The next section of our book talks about ways that you and your parents can work together on making these changes. If you work together it can be a lot of fun, and you will feel very good about yourself when you succeed!

Part Four

Special Projects With
Your Mom or Dad

working on projects with your mom or dad...

Look at your "Things I Want to Change" list on page 60. You might want to pick one of those projects to work on, or there may be some other things you and your parents think of that would make a good project.

- **Pick one project.** You may want to work on several things, but start with just one.

- **Don't pick something hard at first.** Pick something sort of easy and get some practice at learning new behaviors.

- **Don't expect to be perfect. Just try to improve.** Reward yourself each time you succeed, but don't feel discouraged when you don't win a reward. New habits take time to build!

- **Decide with your parents on the rewards you will earn.** Pick a small reward that you can earn each time that you are successful. Pick a larger reward that you can earn at the end of the week if you have been successful for a certain number of days that week.

WEEK # ___ I'M WORKING ON _____

HOW AM I DOING?

	OFF TRACK	GETTING BETTER	SUPER JOB
DAY 1	☐	☐	☐
DAY 2	☐	☐	☐
DAY 3	☐	☐	☐
DAY 4	☐	☐	☐
DAY 5	☐	☐	☐
DAY 6	☐	☐	☐
DAY 7	☐	☐	☐

PROBLEM SOLVING: When I'm trying to _____
but I get off track...

What's the problem? _____

What are some things I can try to solve
the problem?

1.
2.
3.

- **Charting your progress.** Keep a chart of your progress and talk to your mom or dad every day about what went right and what went wrong. On the previous page we have an example of a chart that you and your family can use, or you can make a chart of your own.

Don't expect all "super jobs." Nobody is perfect and nobody changes all at once. If you are having trouble with a special project, sit down with your parents and try to figure out why. Maybe you picked a project that is too hard at first. Maybe you and your parents need better reminders to work on your special project every day.

Good luck with your special projects!

We've covered many things in this book. We hope that you've learned a lot and had some fun, too.

Here's a little reward for all your hard work. Remember, it's always a good idea to reward yourself for a job well done!

Notes to Parents

The more that you know about effective behavior management of children with ADD, the more useful this book will be for you and your child. Here we have listed ways to reward your child, ways to build a positive relationship, organizations that can help, and a suggested reading list.

Ways to Reward Your Child

Changing habits is *hard* work. Kids need incentives (not bribes), just as adults do. Rewards don't have to be expensive. Nor should they be anything you don't want to give your child. They need to be things you both feel good about. Here are some rewards other parents have used.

- Board game with parent
- Bake cookies
- Friend over after school
- Friend for overnight on weekend
- Dinner at McDonalds
- Pizza delivery
- Computer game with parent
- Play ball for 20 minutes with parent
- Not have to do a particular chore one night
- Staying up an extra 15–30 minutes one night
- Get a simple science experiment book and let child select one to do with parent
- Movie rental and popcorn
- Make a special snack with parent
- Plug phone into jack in child's room for a couple of hours
- Grab bag with small favors such as gum, collector cards, vending machine toys—pick one

ALWAYS be generous with social reinforcers:

- Smiles
- Hugs
- Pats on the back
- "I like that"

- "Well done"
- "Thanks"
- "Good try"
- "You're terrific"

These are the real self-esteem builders, even when it does not appear that the child notices.

When you pick a special project with your child, be sure to:

- Be specific about how the checks are earned
- Be specific about how many checks are needed for each reward
- Write these down on the chart so that the rules are clear

Special Time

It is really important for you and your child to have good times together. Everyone feels discouraged if they talk only about problems. Plan a "special time" just for fun each day with your child. It should be a few minutes to be together doing something you both enjoy. Decide together what you want to do. You could play a game, read a book, take a walk, or just talk. It should be fun for both of you—a time to relax, *not* to change behaviors or to learn new things. Don't use the special time as a "reward" that can be gained or lost. When your child is having behavior problems and has been punished or criticized frequently, it is especially important to have "special time" together to rebuild positive feelings between you and your child.

ADD Organizations for Parents

If you are not already a member of CH.A.D.D. (Children and Adults with Attention Deficit Disorder), it may be very useful to you to become a member. CH.A.D.D. is a large national organization, with local chapters in most communities. Local chapters usually host monthly meetings, providing essential information to parents of children with attention problems. To join CH.A.D.D., contact

> CH.A.D.D., 499 Northwest 70th Avenue, Suite 308, Plantation, Florida 33317; (305) 587-3700.

The national CH.A.D.D. office can tell you the location of the CH.A.D.D. chapter nearest you.

Another national organization serving the needs of people with attention problems is ADDA (National Attention Deficit Disorder Association). ADDA focuses particularly on family issues and on the needs of adults with ADD. Since many parents of children with attention problems also struggle with the same issues, and because attention difficulties affect not only the child but the whole family, you may find that ADDA is a very useful organization for you as well. To join ADDA, contact

> Membership Chair, ADDA, 9930 Johnnycake Ridge Road, 3-E, Mentor, OH 44060.

Both of these organizations send newsletters to members, informing them of new books, new research, and new services. We encourage you to join one or both of these organizations. The better informed you are as a parent, the more you will be able to help your child.

Suggested Reading

Here is a reading list you and your child may find helpful

Books, and a Newsletter, for Kids

Brakes: The Interactive Newsletter for Kids with ADD, J. M. Stern and P. O. Quinn, Eds. Magination Press (by subscription).

The Don't Give Up Kid, J. Gehret. Verbal Images Press, 1992.

Eagle Eyes, J. Gehret. Verbal Images Press, 1991.

Keeping A Head In School, M. Levine. Educators Publishing Service, Inc., 1990.

My Brother's a World-Class Pain, M. Gordon. GSI Publications, 1992.

Otto Learns About His Medicine, M. Galvin. Magination Press, 1988.

Putting on the Brakes, P. O. Quinn and J. Stern. Magination Press, 1991.

School Strategies for ADD Teens, K. Nadeau and E. B. Dixon, Chesapeake Psychological Publications, 1993.

Shelly the Hyperactive Turtle, D. Moss. Woodbine House, 1989.

Books for Adults

All Kinds of Minds, M. Levine. Educators Publishing Service, Inc., 1993.

Answers to Distraction, E. M. Hallowell and J. J. Ratey. Pantheon Books, 1994.

Attention Deficit Disorder and Learning Disabilities, B. D. Ingersoll and S. Goldstein. Doubleday, 1993.

Attention Deficit Disorder and the Law, P. S. Latham and P. H. Latham. JKL Publications, 1993.

Attention Deficit Hyperactivity Disorder, R. A. Barkley. Guilford Press, 1990.

Defiant Children, R. A. Barkley. The Guilford Press, 1987.

The Difficult Child, S. Turecki and L. Tanner. Bantam Books, 1989.

Driven to Distraction, E. M. Hallowell and J. J. Ratey. Pantheon Books, 1994.

The Hyperactive Child, Adolescent and Adult, P. H. Wender. Oxford University Press, 1987.

Managing Attention Disorders in Children, S. Goldstein and M. Goldstein. John Wiley and Sons, 1990.

The Misunderstood Child, L. B. Silver. McGraw-Hill, 1984.

Taking Charge of ADHD, R. A. Barkley. Guilford Press, 1995.

Your Hyperactive Child: A Parent's Guide to Coping with Attention Deficit Disorder, B. Ingersoll. Doubleday, 1988.

1-2-3 Magic: Training Your Preschooler and Preteen to Do What You Want Them To Do, T. W. Phelan. Child Management Press, 1995.

About the Authors

Kathleen Nadeau has practiced psychology in the Washington, DC area since 1970. She is the author and coauthor of several books on attention problems for children, adolescents, and adults. Her interest in attention problems is personal as well as professional. Having raised a child with attention difficulties, she hopes that this book will make the going easier for children growing up today.

Ellen Dixon has been a psychotherapist for over twenty-five years, specializing in the everyday adjustment problems of children and adults and in the diagnosis and treatment of attention deficit-related problems. She has helped hundreds of families understand and better cope with attention disorders. Ellen works in an office with two desks and a credenza, which helps to keep her own attention and organization problems under better control.

John Rose is an award-winning cartoonist whose work is syndicated throughout Virginia and has been reprinted in *The Washington Times, The Washington Post National Weekly Edition,* and the *National Forum.* For several years, his work has been featured in *The Best Editorial Cartoons of the Year* collections. John has written and illustrated two books: *Cartoons that Fill the Bill,* a collection of cartoons about Bill Clinton, and *Fun with Pup,* a children's cartoon/activity book based on his children's cartoon page, "Kids' Home Newspaper." His cartoons can be found displayed on refrigerators everywhere.